Term Service Short Contract

This contract should be used for the appointment of a supplier for a period of time to manage and provide a service.
The NEC3 Term Service Short Contract is an alternative to the NEC3 Term Service Contract and is for use with contracts which do not require sophisticated management techniques, comprise straightforward work and impose only low risks on both the Employer and the Contractor

An NEC document

April 2013

Construction Clients' Board endorsement of NEC3

The Construction Clients' Board recommends that public sector organisations use the NEC3 contracts when procuring construction. Standardising use of this comprehensive suite of contracts should help to deliver efficiencies across the public sector and promote behaviours in line with the principles of *Achieving Excellence in Construction*.

Facilities Management Board support for NEC3

The Facilities Management Board recognises that the NEC Term Service Contracts support good practice in FM Procurement in the public sector.

Cabinet Office UK

supported by

ADVANCING OUR PROFESSION

BIFM recommends the use of
NEC3 Term Service Contract and
NEC3 Term Service Short Contract for all types
of Facilities Management and maintenance contracts.

NEC is a division of Thomas Telford Ltd, which is a wholly owned subsidiary of the Institution of Civil Engineers (ICE), the owner and developer of the NEC.

The NEC is a family of standard contracts, each of which has these characteristics:

- Its use stimulates good management of the relationship between the two parties to the contract and, hence, of the work included in the contract.
- It can be used in a wide variety of commercial situations, for a wide variety of types of work and in any location.
- It is a clear and simple document – using language and a structure which are straightforward and easily understood.

NEC3 Term Service Short Contract is one of the NEC family and is consistent with all other NEC3 documents. Also available are the Term Service Short Contract Guidance Notes and Flow Charts.

ISBN (complete box set) 978 0 7277 5867 5
ISBN (this document) 978 0 7277 5893 4
ISBN (Term Service Short Contract Guidance Notes and Flow Charts) 978 0 7277 5929 0

First edition 2008
Reprinted 2009, 2010
Reprinted with amendments 2013

British Library Cataloguing in Publication Data for this publication is available from the British Library.

Typeset by Academic + Technical, Bristol

Printed and bound in Great Britain by Bell & Bain Limited, Glasgow, UK

FOREWORD

I was delighted to be asked to write the Foreword for the NEC3 Contracts.

I have followed the outstanding rise and success of NEC contracts for a number of years now, in particular during my tenure as the 146th President of the Institution of Civil Engineers, 2010/11.

In my position as UK Government's Chief Construction Adviser, I am working with Government and industry to ensure Britain's construction sector is equipped with the knowledge, skills and best practice it needs in its transition to a low carbon economy. I am promoting innovation in the sector, including in particular the use of Building Information Modelling (BIM) in public sector construction procurement; and the synergy and fit with the collaborative nature of NEC contracts is obvious. The Government's construction strategy is a very significant investment and NEC contracts will play an important role in setting high standards of contract preparation, management and the desirable behaviour of our industry.

In the UK, we are faced with having to deliver a 15–20 per cent reduction in the cost to the public sector of construction during the lifetime of this Parliament. Shifting mind-set, attitude and behaviour into best practice NEC processes will go a considerable way to achieving this.

Of course, NEC contracts are used successfully around the world in both public and private sector projects; this trend seems set to continue at an increasing pace. NEC contracts are, according to my good friend and NEC's creator Dr Martin Barnes CBE, about better management of projects. This is quite achievable and I encourage you to understand NEC contracts to the best you can and exploit the potential this offers us all.

Peter Hansford

UK Government's Chief Construction Adviser
Cabinet Office

The NEC contracts are the only suite of standard contracts designed to facilitate and encourage good management of the projects on which they are used. The experience of using NEC contracts around the world is that they really make a difference. Previously, standard contracts were written mainly as legal documents best left in the desk drawer until costly and delaying problems had occurred and there were lengthy arguments about who was to blame.

The language of NEC contracts is clear and simple, and the procedures set out are all designed to stimulate good management. Foresighted collaboration between all the contributors to the project is the aim. The contracts set out how the interfaces between all the organisations involved will be managed – from the client through the designers and main contractors to all the many subcontractors and suppliers.

Versions of the NEC contract are specific to the work of professional service providers such as project managers and designers, to main contractors, to subcontractors and to suppliers. The wide range of situations covered by the contracts means that they do not need to be altered to suit any particular situation.

The NEC contracts are the first to deal specifically and effectively with management of the inevitable risks and uncertainties which are encountered to some extent on all projects. Management of the expected is easy, effective management of the unexpected draws fully on the collaborative approach inherent in the NEC contracts.

Most people working on projects using the NEC contracts for the first time are hugely impressed by the difference between the confrontational characteristics of traditional contracts and the teamwork engendered by the NEC. The NEC does not include specific provisions for dispute avoidance. They are not necessary. Collaborative management itself is designed to avoid disputes and it really works.

It is common for the final account for the work on a project to be settled at the time when the work is finished. The traditional long period of expensive professional work after completion to settle final payments just is not needed.

The NEC contracts are truly a massive change for the better for the industries in which they are used.

Dr Martin Barnes CBE

Originator of the NEC contracts

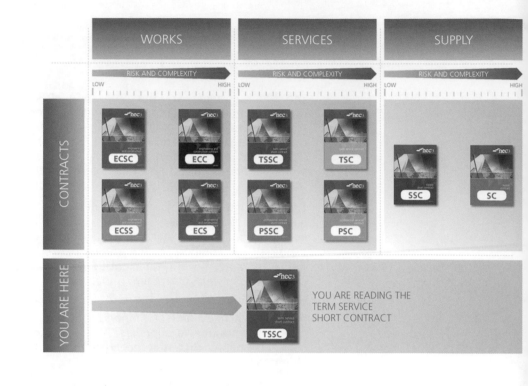

ACKNOWLEDGEMENTS

The first edition of the Term Service Short Contract was produced by the Institution of Civil Engineers through its NEC Panel. It was mainly drafted by Bill Weddell based on work by Andrew Baird.

The Flow Charts were produced by Ross Hayes.

The original NEC was designed and drafted by Dr Martin Barnes then of Coopers and Lybrand with the assistance of Professor J. G. Perry then of The University of Birmingham, T. W. Weddell then of Travers Morgan Management, T. H. Nicholson, Consultant to the Institution of Civil Engineers, A. Norman then of the University of Manchester Institute of Science and Technology and P. A. Baird, then Corporate Contracts Consultant, Eskom, South Africa.

The members of the NEC Panel are:

N. C. Shaw, FCIPS, CEng, MIMechE (Chairman)
P. A. Baird, BSc, CEng, FICE, M(SA)ICE, MAPM
A. J. M. Blackler, BA, LLB(Cantab), MCIArb
M. Codling, BSc, ICIOB, MAPM
L. T. Eames, BSc, FRICS, FCIOB
M. Garratt, BSc(Hons), MRICS, FCIArb
J. J. Lofty, MRICS

NEC Consultant:

R. A. Gerrard, BSc(Hons), FRICS, FCIArb, FCInstCES

Secretariat:

J. M. Hawkins, BA(Hons), MSc
S. Hernandez, BSc, MSc

AMENDMENTS APRIL 2013

The following amendments have been made to the September 2008 edition. Full details of all amendments are available on www.neccontract.com.

Page	Clause	Line	
3			Last paragraph replace: 'September 2008 with 'April 2013'
CC 2	14.2	2	at end of sentence add: 'or a Task Order'
	14.8	3	Add: 'The *Contractor* does the work so that a Task is completed on or before the Task Completion Date.'
CC 5	51.1	1	replace: 'The *Contractor* pays' with 'Each payment is made'
	60.1	1	add: clauses '60.1(6)' and '60.1(7)' new clause
	62.2		'62.2' now '62.3'
			'62.3' now '62.4'
CC 6	63.3		new clause
	63.4		new clause
	63.5		new clause
	63.6		old clause '63.3'
CC 9	90.4	1	replace: 'made a payment' with 'paid an amount due under the contract'
CC 11			Delete 94.1 and insert new clause 1.1 to 1.8

nec®3 Term Service

Short Contract

A contract between ....

....

....

and ....

....

for ....

....

....

contract forms

conditions of contract

Contents   Page

> **Notes about this contract are printed in boxes like this one. They are not part of the contract.**

1

Contract Data

The *Employer* is

Name ....

Address ....

Telephone ....

E-mail address ....

If the *Employer* appoints an *Employer*'s *Agent*, the *Employer*'s *Agent* is

Name ....

Address ....

Telephone ....

E-mail address ....

The authority of the *Employer*'s *Agent*, is

....

....

The *service* is ....

....

The *starting date* is ....

The *service period* is .... months.

The *period for reply* is .... weeks.

The *assessment day* is the .... of each month.

Does the United Kingdom Housing Grants, Construction and Regeneration Act (1996) apply?   Yes / No (delete as appropriate)

contract forms

conditions of contract

2

Contract Data

The *Adjudicator* is

Name ....

Address ....

Telephone ....

E-mail address ....

The interest rate on late payment is .... % per complete week of delay.

> Insert a rate only if a rate less than 0.5% per week of delay has been agreed.

The *Contractor* is not liable to the *Employer* for loss of or damage to the *Employer*'s

property in excess of .... for any one event.

The *Employer* provides this insurance

> Only enter details here if the *Employer* is to provide insurance.

....

....

The minimum amount of cover for the first insurance stated in the

Insurance Table is ....

The minimum amount of cover for the third insurance stated in the

Insurance Table is ....

The minimum amount of cover for the fourth insurance stated in the

Insurance Table is ....

The *Adjudicator nominating body* is ....

The *tribunal* is ....

If the *tribunal* is arbitration, the arbitration procedure is ....

The *conditions of contract* are the NEC3 Term Service Short Contract April 2013 and the following additional conditions

> Only enter details here if additional conditions are required.

....

3

The *Contractor*'s Offer

The *Contractor* is

Name ....

Address ....

....

Telephone ....

E-mail address ....

The percentage for overheads and profit added to the Defined Cost for people is .... %.

The percentage for overheads and profit added to other Defined Cost is .... %.

The *Contractor* offers to Provide the Service in accordance with the *conditions of contract* for an amount to be determined in accordance with the *conditions of contract*.

The offered total of the Prices for part of ....
the *service* in Part 1 of the Price List is

The offered total of the Prices for part of ....
the *service* in Part 2 of the Price List is

Enter the total of the Prices from the Price List.

Signed on behalf of the *Contractor*

Name ....

Position ....

Signature .... Date ....

The *Employer*'s Acceptance

The *Employer* accepts the *Contractor*'s Offer to Provide the Service

Signed on behalf of the *Employer*

Name ....

Position ....

Signature .... Date ....

www.neccontract.com

contract forms

conditions of contract

Price List

The Price List is in two parts. Part 1 is for work described in the Service Information not requiring the *Employer* to issue a Task Order. Part 2 is for work to be carried out within a stated period of time on a Task by Task basis and instructed by Task Order. The *service* may comprise work under Part 1 only or Part 2 only or a mix of both.

Entries in the first four columns of Part 1 of the Price List are made either by the *Employer* or the tenderer. Entries in the first four columns of Part 2 of the Price List would normally be made by the *Employer* as the Party most likely to know the kind of work which will be instructed by the issue of Task Orders. The tenderer then enters a rate for each item and multiplies it by the Expected quantity to produce the Price to be entered in the final column.

If the *Contractor* is to be paid an amount for the item which is not adjusted if the quantity of work in the item changes, the tenderer enters the amount in the Price column only, the Unit, Expected quantity and Rate columns being left blank.

If the *Contractor* is to be paid an amount for the item of work which is the rate for the work multiplied by the quantity completed, the tenderer enters a rate for each item and multiplies it by the Expected quantity to produce the Price, to be entered in the final column.

If the *Contractor* is to be paid a Price for an item proportional to the length of time for which a service is provided, a unit of time is stated in the Unit column and the expected length of time (as a quantity of the stated units of time) is stated in the Expected quantity column.

The rates and Prices entered for each item includes for all work and other things necessary to complete the item.

PART 1

Item number	Description	Unit	Expected quantity	Rate	Price
. . . .	. . . .	. . . .	. . . .	. . . .	. . . .
. . . .	. . . .	. . . .	. . . .	. . . .	. . . .
. . . .	. . . .	. . . .	. . . .	. . . .	. . . .

The total of the Prices for Part 1

PART 2

Item number	Description	Unit	Expected quantity	Rate	Price
. . . .	. . . .	. . . .	. . . .	. . . .	. . . .
. . . .	. . . .	. . . .	. . . .	. . . .	. . . .
. . . .	. . . .	. . . .	. . . .	. . . .	. . . .

The total of the Prices for Part 2

5

Service Information

The Service Information should be a complete and precise statement of the *Employer*'s requirements. If it is incomplete or imprecise there is a risk that the *Contractor* will interpret it differently from the *Employer*'s intention. The Service Information should state clearly the part of the *service* which is to be carried out by the *Contractor* and which does not require the *Employer* to issue a Task Order. This part of the *service* is priced in Part 1 of the Price List. Information provided by the *Contractor* should be listed in the Service Information only if the *Employer* is satisfied that it is required, is part of a complete statement of the *Employer*'s requirements and is consistent with the other parts of the Service Information.

1 Description of the *service*

Give a detailed description of what the *Contractor* is required to do. This may include drawings.

....

....

....

....

....

....

....

2 Specifications

List the specifications that apply to this contract.

Title	Date or revision	Tick if publicly available
....	....	....
....	....	....
....	....	....
....	....	....
....	....	....
....	....	....
....	....	....

6

contract forms

conditions of contract

Service Information

3 Constraints on how the *Contractor* Provides the Service

> State any constraints on the sequence and timing of work and on the methods and conduct of work including the requirements for any work by the *Employer*.

. . . .

. . . .

. . . .

. . . .

. . . .

. . . .

. . . .

. . . .

4 Requirements for the plan

> State whether a plan is required and, if it is, state what form it is to be in, what information is to be shown on it, when it is to be submitted and when it is to be updated.

. . . .

. . . .

. . . .

. . . .

. . . .

. . . .

. . . .

. . . .

. . . .

Service Information

5 Services and other things provided by the *Employer*

> Describe what the *Employer* will provide, such as services (including water and electricity) and "free issue" plant and materials and equipment.

Item	Date by which it will be provided
....	....
....	....
....	....
....	....
....	....
....	....
....	....
....	....
....	....
....	....
....	....
....	....
....	....
....	....
....	....
....	....
....	....
....	....
....	....
....	....

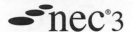

Service Information

6 Property affected by the *service*

> Give information about any property affected by the *service* and any other information which is likely to affect the *Contractor*'s work.

....

....

....

....

....

....

....

....

....

....

....

....

....

....

....

....

....

....

....

....

....

....

contract forms

conditions of contract

Task Order

Task Order form for use when work within the *service* is instructed to be carried out within a stated time period of time on a Task by Task basis

Task Order No .... *service* ....

To ....

.... *(Contractor)*

I propose to instruct you to carry out the following task

Description ....

....

....

Starting date ....

Completion date ....

Delay damages per week ....

....

Please submit your price and programme proposals below.

Signed .... Date ....

(for *Employer*)

Total of Prices for items of work on the
Price List   (details attached)

....

Total of Prices for items of work not on the
Price List   (details attached)

_____

Total of the Prices

The programme for the Task is .... [ref] (attached)

Signed .... Date ....

(for *Contractor*)

I accept the above price and programme and instruct you to carry out the Task

Signed .... Date ....

(for *Employer*)

10

CONDITIONS OF CONTRACT

1 General

Actions **10**

10.1 The *Employer* and the *Contractor* shall act as stated in this contract and in a spirit of mutual trust and co-operation.

Identified and **11**
defined terms

11.1 In the *conditions of contract*, terms identified in the Contract Data are in italics and defined terms have capital initials.

11.2 (1) A Defect is a part of the *service* which is not in accordance with the Service Information.

(2) Defined Cost is the amount paid by the *Contractor* in Providing the Service (excluding any tax which the *Contractor* can recover) for

- people employed by the *Contractor*,
- plant and materials,
- work subcontracted by the *Contractor* and
- equipment.

The amount for equipment includes amounts paid for hired equipment and an amount for the use of equipment owned by the *Contractor* which is the amount the *Contractor* would have paid if the equipment had been hired.

(3) The Parties are the *Employer* and the *Contractor*.

(4) The Prices are the amounts stated in the Price column of the Price List. Where a quantity is stated for an item in the Price List, the Price is calculated by multiplying the quantity by the rate.

(5) To Provide the Service means to do the work necessary to provide the *service* in accordance with this contract and all incidental work, services and actions which this contract requires.

(6) Service Information is information which either

- specifies and describes the *service* or
- states any constraints on how the *Contractor* Provides the Service

and is either

- in the document called 'Service Information' or
- in an instruction given in accordance with this contract.

(7) A Task is work within the *service* which the *Employer* may instruct the *Contractor* to carry out within a stated period of time.

(8) A Task Order is the *Employer*'s instruction to carry out a Task.

(9) Task Completion Date is the date for completion stated in a Task Order unless later changed in accordance with this contract.

www.neccontract.com

contract data

conditions of contract

Interpretation and the Law   **12**

12.1   In this contract, except where the context shows otherwise, words in the singular also mean in the plural and the other way round and words in the masculine also mean in the feminine and neuter.

12.2   This contract is governed by the law of the country in which the *service* is provided.

12.3   No change to this contract, unless provided for by the *conditions of contract*, has effect unless it has been agreed, confirmed in writing and signed by the Parties.

12.4   This contract is the entire agreement between the Parties.

Communications   **13**

13.1   Each communication which this contract requires has effect when it is received in writing at the last address notified by the recipient for receiving communications.

13.2   If this contract requires the *Employer* or the *Contractor* to reply to a communication, unless otherwise stated in this contract, he replies within the *period for reply*.

The *Employer*'s authority, delegation and *Employer*'s Agent   **14**

14.1   The *Contractor* obeys an instruction which is in accordance with this contract and is given to him by the *Employer*.

14.2   The *Employer* may give an instruction to the *Contractor* which changes the Service Information or a Task Order.

14.3   The *Employer*'s acceptance of a communication from the *Contractor* or of his work does not change the *Contractor*'s responsibility to Provide the Service.

14.4   The *Employer*, after notifying the *Contractor*, may delegate any of the *Employer*'s actions and may cancel any delegation. A reference to an action of the *Employer* in this contract includes an action by his delegate.

14.5   If the *Employer*'s *Agent* is not identified in the Contract Data, the *Employer* may appoint one after notifying the *Contractor* of his name. The *Employer*'s *Agent* acts on behalf of the *Employer* with the authority set out in the Contract Data. The *Employer* may replace the *Employer*'s *Agent* after he has notified the *Contractor* of the name of the replacement.

14.6   During the *service period* the *Employer* may issue a proposed Task Order to the *Contractor*. The *Contractor* prices each proposed Task Order using the rates and prices from the Price List and submits it with a Task programme, to the *Employer* for acceptance. Prices for work not included in the Price List are assessed in the same way as compensation events. The *Employer* consults the *Contractor* about the contents of a Task Order before he accepts and issues it.

14.7   A Task Order includes

- a detailed description of the work in the Task,
- a priced and totalled list of the items of work in the Task,
- the starting and completion dates for the Task and
- the amount of delay damages for the Task.

14.8   The *Contractor* does not start a Task until the *Employer* has accepted the priced Task Order and programme, and instructed the *Contractor* to carry out the Task. The *Contractor* does the work so that a Task is completed on or before the Task Completion Date. Prices for work not already included in the Price List are added to the Price List.

Employer **provides right of** **access and things**	**15**	
	15.1	The *Employer* provides a right of access for the *Contractor* as necessary for the work included in this contract.
	15.2	The *Employer* provides things which he is to provide as stated in the Service Information.
Early warning	**16**	
	16.1	The *Contractor* and the *Employer* give an early warning by notifying the other as soon as either becomes aware of any matter which could

- increase the total of the Prices,
- interfere with the timing of the *service* or
- impair the effectiveness of the *service*.

The *Contractor* may give an early warning by notifying the *Employer* of any other matter which could increase his total cost. Early warning of a matter for which a compensation event has previously been notified is not required.

16.2 The *Contractor* and the *Employer* co-operate in making and considering proposals for how the effect of each matter which has been notified as an early warning can be avoided or reduced and deciding and recording actions to be taken.

2 The *Contractor*'s main responsibilities

Providing the Service	**20**	
	20.1	The *Contractor* Provides the Service in accordance with the Service Information and minimises the interference caused by his work, to the *Employer* and others.
Subcontracting and people	**21**	
	21.1	If the *Contractor* subcontracts work, he is responsible for Providing the Service as if he had not subcontracted.
	21.2	This contract applies as if a subcontractor's employees and equipment were the *Contractor*'s.
	21.3	The *Employer* may, having stated reasons, instruct the *Contractor* to remove an employee. The *Contractor* then arranges that, after one day, the employee has no further connection with the work included in this contract.

3 Time

Starting and the ***service period***	**30**	
	30.1	The *Contractor* does not start work until the *starting date* and Provides the Service until the later of the end of the *service period* and the latest Task Completion Date.
Instructions to stop or **not to start work**	**31**	
	31.1	The *Employer* may instruct the *Contractor* to stop or not to start any work and may later instruct him to re-start or start it.
The *Contractor*'s plan	**32**	
	32.1	The *Contractor* submits plans to the *Employer* for acceptance as stated in the Service Information.

4 Testing and Defects

Tests and inspections **40**

40.1 The *Employer* and the *Contractor* carry out tests and inspections required by the Service Information.

Notifying Defects **41**

41.1 The *Employer* may notify a Defect at any time before the later of the end of the *service period* and the latest date for completion of a Task.

Correcting Defects **42**

42.1 The *Contractor* corrects Defects whether notified or not, within a time which minimises the adverse effect on the *Employer* and others.

42.2 The *Employer* allows the *Contractor* access if it is needed for correcting a Defect.

Accepting Defects **43**

43.1 The *Contractor* and the *Employer* may each propose to the other that the Service Information should be changed so that a Defect does not have to be corrected. If the *Contractor* and the *Employer* are prepared to consider the change, the *Contractor* submits a quotation for reduced Prices to the *Employer* for acceptance. If the *Employer* accepts the quotation, he gives an instruction to change the Service Information and the Prices accordingly.

Uncorrected Defects **44**

44.1 If the *Contractor* has not corrected a notified Defect within the time required by this contract, the *Employer* assesses the cost of having the Defect corrected by others and the *Contractor* pays this amount.

5 Payment

Assessing the amount due **50**

50.1 The *Contractor* assesses the amount due and, by each *assessment day*, applies to the *Employer* for payment of the change in the amount due since the last payment. There is an *assessment day* in each month from the *starting date* until the month after the later of the end of the *service period* and the latest date for completion of a Task.

50.2 The amount due is

- the Price for each lump sum item in the Price List or Task Order which the *Contractor* has completed,
- where a quantity is stated for an item in the Price List or Task Order, an amount calculated by multiplying the quantity which the *Contractor* has completed by the rate,
- any tax which the law requires the *Employer* to pay to the *Contractor* and
- other amounts to be paid to the *Contractor*, less
- amounts to be paid by or retained from the *Contractor*.

50.3 The *Employer* corrects any wrongly assessed amount due and notifies the *Contractor* of the correction before paying the *Contractor*.

50.4 The *Contractor* pays delay damages for each Task which has not been completed by the Task Completion Date. The delay damages are at the rate stated in the Task Order calculated from the Task Completion Date until completion of the Task.

Payment	**51**	
	51.1	Each payment is made within three weeks after the next *assessment day* which follows receipt of an application for payment by the *Contractor*.
	51.2	Interest is paid if a payment is late or includes a correction of an earlier payment. Interest is assessed from the date by which the correct payment should have been made until the date when it is paid. Interest is calculated at the rate stated in the Contract Data or, if none is stated, at 0.5% of the delayed amount per complete week of delay.

6 Compensation events

Compensation events **60**

60.1 The following are compensation events.

(1) The *Employer* gives an instruction changing the Service Information unless the change is in order to make a Defect acceptable.

(2) The *Employer* does not provide

- a right of access or
- other things which he is to provide as stated in the Service Information.

(3) The *Employer* gives an instruction to stop or not to start any work unless the instruction arises from a fault of the *Contractor*.

(4) The *Employer* does not reply to a communication from the *Contractor* within the period required by this contract.

(5) The *Employer* changes a decision which he has previously communicated to the *Contractor*.

(6) The *Employer* does not work in accordance with a Task Programme or within the conditions stated in the Service Information.

(7) The *Employer* gives an instruction changing a Task Order.

Notifying compensation **61**
events 61.1 The *Contractor* notifies the *Employer* of an event which has happened or which he expects to happen as a compensation event. If the *Contractor* does not notify a compensation event within four weeks of becoming aware of the event, he is not entitled to a change in the Prices or a Task Completion Date unless the event arises from an instruction of the *Employer*.

61.2 The *Employer* notifies the *Contractor* of his decision whether the event is a compensation event within one week of the *Contractor*'s notification to the *Employer* of the event. If the *Employer* agrees that the event is a compensation event, he includes with his notification an instruction to the *Contractor* to submit a quotation for the event.

Quotations for **62**
compensation events 62.1 A quotation for a compensation event comprises proposed changes to the Prices or rates assessed by the *Contractor*. The assessment of a change to a Task Order may include a proposed change to the Task Completion Date. The *Contractor* submits details of his assessment with each quotation. The *Contractor* submits a quotation within two weeks of being instructed to do so by the *Employer* or, if no such instruction is received, within three weeks of the notification of a compensation event.

62.2 If the *Contractor* does not provide a quotation for a compensation event within the time allowed, the *Employer* assesses the compensation event and notifies the *Contractor* of his assessment.

62.3   The *Employer* replies within two weeks of the *Contractor*'s submission accepting or disagreeing with the quotation.

62.4   If the *Employer* does not agree with the quotation, the *Contractor* may submit a revised quotation within two weeks of the *Employer*'s reply. If the *Employer* does not agree with the revised quotation or if none is received, the *Employer* assesses the compensation event and notifies the *Contractor* of his assessment.

Assessing compensation events   **63**

63.1   For a compensation event which affects only the quantities of work shown in the Price List, the change to the Prices is assessed by multiplying the changed quantities of work by the appropriate rates in the Price List.

63.2   For other compensation events, the changes to the Prices are assessed by forecasting the effect of a compensation event upon the Defined Cost or, if the compensation event has already occurred, the assessment is based upon the Defined Cost due to the event which the *Contractor* has incurred. Effects on Defined Cost are assessed at open market or competitively tendered prices with deductions for all discounts, rebates and taxes which can be recovered. Effects on Defined Cost are assessed separately for

- people employed by the *Contractor*,
- plant and materials,
- work subcontracted by the *Contractor* and
- equipment.

The *Contractor* shows how each of these effects is built up in each quotation for a compensation event. The percentages for overheads and profit stated in the *Contractor*'s Offer are applied to the assessed effect of the event on the Defined Cost.

63.3   A delay to a Task Completion Date is assessed as the length of time that, due to the compensation event, completion of the Task is forecast to be delayed.

63.4   The cost of preparing quotations for compensation events is not included in the assessment of compensation events.

63.5   Assessments for changed Prices for compensation events are in the form of changes to the Price List.

63.6   The assessment of a compensation event is not revised if a forecast upon which it is based is shown by later recorded information to have been wrong.

7 Use of equipment and things

The Parties' use of equipment and things   **70**

70.1   The *Contractor* has the right to use equipment and other things provided by the *Employer* only to Provide the Service.

70.2   At the later of the end of the *service period* and the latest date for completion of a Task, the *Contractor*

- returns to the *Employer*, equipment and surplus things provided by the *Employer*,
- provides items of equipment for the *Employer*'s use as stated in the Service Information and
- provides information and other things for the *Employer*'s use as stated in the Service Information.

8 Indemnity, insurance and liability

Limitation of liability **80**

80.1 For any one event, the liability of the *Contractor* to the *Employer* for loss of or damage to the *Employer*'s property is limited to the amount stated in the Contract Data.

80.2 The *Contractor* is not liable to the *Employer* for the *Employer*'s indirect or consequential loss except as provided for in the *conditions of contract*.

80.3 Exclusion or limitation of liability applies in contract, tort or delict and otherwise and to the maximum extent permitted in law.

Indemnities **81**

81.1 The *Employer* indemnifies the *Contractor* against claims, proceedings, compensation and costs payable which are the unavoidable result of the *service* or of Providing the Service or which arise from

- fault,
- negligence,
- breach of statutory duty,
- infringement of an intellectual property right or
- interference with a legal right

by the *Employer* or by a person employed by or contracted to the *Employer* except the *Contractor*.

81.2 The *Contractor* indemnifies the *Employer* against other

- losses and claims in respect of
  - death of or injury to a person and
  - loss of and damage to property (other than the *Employer*'s property) and
- claims, proceedings, compensation and costs payable arising from or in connection with the *Contractor*'s Providing the Service.

81.3 The liability of each Party to indemnify the other is reduced to the extent that events which are the other Party's responsibility contributed to the losses, claims, proceedings, compensation and costs.

Insurance cover **82**

82.1 The *Contractor* provides, in the joint names of the Parties and from the *starting date* until the later of the end of the *service period* and the latest date for completion of a Task, the insurances stated in the Insurance Table. The *Contractor* does not provide an insurance which the *Employer* is to provide as stated in the Contract Data.

contract data

conditions of contract

INSURANCE TABLE

Insurance against	Minimum amount of cover or minimum limit of indemnity
Loss of or damage caused by the *Contractor* to the *Employer*'s property	The amount stated in the Contract Data
Loss of or damage to equipment, plant and materials	The replacement cost
The *Contractor*'s liability for loss of or damage to property (except the *Employer*'s property, equipment and other things used to Provide the Service) and for bodily injury to or death of a person (not an employee of the *Contractor*) arising from or in connection with the *Contractor*'s Providing the Service	The amount stated in the Contract Data for any one event with cross liability so that the insurance applies to the Parties separately
Liability for death of or bodily injury to employees of the *Contractor* arising out of and in the course of their employment in connection with this contract	The greater of the amount required by the applicable law and the amount stated in the Contract Data for any one event

9 Termination and dispute resolution

Termination and reasons for termination

90

90.1 If either Party wishes to terminate the *Contractor*'s obligation to Provide the Service, he notifies the other Party giving details of his reason for terminating. The *Employer* issues a termination certificate promptly if the reason complies with this contract. After a termination certificate has been issued, the *Contractor* does no further work necessary to Provide the Service.

90.2 Either Party may terminate if the other Party has become insolvent or its equivalent (Reason 1).

90.3 The *Employer* may terminate if the *Employer* has notified the *Contractor* that the *Contractor* has defaulted in one of the following ways and the *Contractor* has not stopped defaulting within two weeks of the notification.

- Substantially failed to comply with this contract (Reason 2).
- Substantially hindered the *Employer* (Reason 3).
- Substantially broken a health or safety regulation (Reason 4).

The *Employer* may terminate for any other reason (Reason 5).

90.4 The *Contractor* may terminate if

- the *Employer* has not paid an amount due under the contract within ten weeks of the *assessment day* which followed receipt of the *Contractor*'s application for payment (Reason 6) or
- the *Employer* has instructed the *Contractor* to stop or not to start any substantial work or all work for a reason which is not the *Contractor*'s fault and an instruction allowing the work to re-start or start has not been given within eight weeks (Reason 7).

90.5   The *Employer* may terminate if an event which the Parties could not reasonably prevent has substantially affected the *Contractor*'s work for a continuous period of more than thirteen weeks (Reason 8).

Procedures on termination   91

91.1   On termination, the *Employer* may complete the *service* himself or employ other people to do so. The *Contractor* leaves the area affected by the *Contractor*'s work and removes his equipment.

91.2   On termination, the *Contractor*

- returns to the *Employer*, equipment and surplus things provided by the *Employer*
- provides items of equipment for the *Employer*'s use as stated in the Service Information and
- provides information and other things for the *Employer*'s use as stated in the Service Information.

Payment on termination   92

92.1   The amount due on termination includes

- an amount due assessed as for normal payments,
- the cost of plant and materials which have been delivered and retained by the *Employer* or which the *Employer* owns and of which the *Contractor* has to accept delivery and
- any amounts retained by the *Employer*.

92.2   If the *Employer* terminates for Reason 1, 2, 3 or 4, the amount due on termination also includes a deduction of the forecast additional cost to the *Employer* of completing the *service*.

92.3   If the *Contractor* terminates for Reason 1, 6 or 7 or if the *Employer* terminates for Reason 5, the amount due on termination also includes 5% of any excess of a forecast of the amount due on the last *assessment day* had there been no termination over the amount due on termination assessed as for normal payments.

Dispute resolution   93

93.1   A dispute arising under or in connection with this contract is referred to and decided by the *Adjudicator*.

The *Adjudicator*   93.2

(1) The Parties appoint the *Adjudicator* under the NEC Adjudicators Contract current at the *starting date*. The *Adjudicator* acts impartially and decides the dispute as an independent adjudicator and not as an arbitrator.

(2) If the *Adjudicator* is not identified in the Contract Data or if the *Adjudicator* resigns or is unable to act, the Parties choose a new adjudicator jointly. If the Parties have not chosen an adjudicator, either Party may ask the *Adjudicator nominating body* to choose one. The *Adjudicator nominating body* chooses an adjudicator within four days of the request. The chosen adjudicator becomes the *Adjudicator*.

(3) The *Adjudicator*, his employees and agents are not liable to the Parties for any action or failure to take action in an adjudication unless the action or failure to take action was in bad faith.

The adjudication   93.3

(1) A Party may refer a dispute to the *Adjudicator* if

- the Party notified the other Party of the dispute within four weeks of becoming aware of it and
- between two and four further weeks have passed since the notification.

If a disputed matter is not notified and referred within the times set out in this contract, neither Party may subsequently refer it to the *Adjudicator* or the *tribunal*.

contract data

conditions of contract

(2) The Party referring the dispute to the *Adjudicator* includes with his referral information to be considered by the *Adjudicator*. Any more information is provided within two weeks of the referral. This period may be extended if the *Adjudicator* and the Parties agree.

(3) The *Adjudicator* may take the initiative in ascertaining the facts and the law related to the dispute. He may instruct a Party to take any other action which he considers necessary to reach his decision and to do so within a stated time.

(4) A communication between a Party and the *Adjudicator* is communicated to the other Party at the same time.

(5) If the *Adjudicator's* decision includes assessment of additional cost or delay caused to the *Contractor*, he makes his assessment in the same way as a compensation event is assessed.

(6) The *Adjudicator* decides the dispute and notifies the Parties of his decision and his reasons within four weeks of the referral. This period may be extended by up to two weeks with the consent of the referring Party, or by any period agreed by the Parties.

If the *Adjudicator* does not notify his decision within the time allowed, either Party may act as if the *Adjudicator* has resigned.

(7) Unless and until the *Adjudicator* has notified the Parties of his decision, the Parties proceed as if the matter disputed was not disputed.

(8) The *Adjudicator's* decision is binding on the Parties unless and until revised by the *tribunal* and is enforceable as a matter of contractual obligation between the Parties and not as an arbitral award. The *Adjudicator's* decision is final and binding if neither Party has notified the other within the times required by this contract that he intends to refer the matter to the *tribunal*.

Review by the *tribunal* 93.4 A Party may refer a dispute to the *tribunal* if

- the Party is dissatisfied with the *Adjudicator's* decision or
- the *Adjudicator* did not notify a decision within the time allowed and a new adjudicator has not been chosen,

except that neither Party may refer a dispute to the *tribunal* unless they have notified the other Party of their intention to do so not more than four weeks after the end of the time allowed for the *Adjudicator's* decision.

If the United Kingdom Housing Grants, Construction and Regeneration Act 1996 as amended by the Local Democracy, Economic Development and Construction Act 2009 (the Act) applies to this contract, the following additional conditions apply.

Definitions	1.1	(1) The payment due date for an application for payment by the *Contractor* is the *assessment day* which follows receipt of that application.
		(2) The final date for payment is three weeks after the payment due date.
Assessing the amount due	1.2	The *Contractor*'s application for payment is the notice of payment specifying the sum that the *Contractor* considers to be due at the payment due date (the notified sum). The *Contractor*'s application states the basis on which the amount is calculated and includes details of the calculation.
	1.3	The following replaces clause 50.3
		If the *Employer* intends to pay less than the notified sum, he notifies the *Contractor* of the amount which the *Employer* considers to be due not later than seven days (the prescribed period) before the final date for payment. The *Employer*'s notification states the basis on which the amount is calculated and includes details of the calculation. A Party pays the notified sum unless he has notified his intention to pay less than the notified sum.
Compensation event	1.4	If the *Contractor* exercises his right under the Act to suspend performance, it is a compensation event.
The adjudication	1.5	The following replaces clause 93.3(1)
		A Party may issue to the other Party a notice of his intention to refer a dispute to adjudication at any time. He refers the dispute to the *Adjudicator* within one week of the notice.
	1.6	The *Adjudicator* may in his decision allocate his fees and expenses between the Parties.
	1.7	The *Adjudicator* may, within five days of giving his decision to the Parties, correct the decision to remove a clerical or typographical error arising by accident or omission.
	1.8	If the *Adjudicator*'s decision changes an amount notified as due, payment of the sum decided by the *Adjudicator* is due not later than seven days from the date of the decision or the final date for payment of the notified amount, whichever is the later.

contract data

conditions of contract

nec³ Term Service Short Contract

Contract Forms are indexed by Page number with a prefix p. Conditions of Contract (CC) are indexed by clause numbers (main clause heads by **bold numbers**). Terms in *italics* are identified in Contract Data, and defined terms have capital initial letters.